THE HOME FRONT

Liz Gogerly
Photographs by Martyn F. Chillmaid

RECONSTRUCTED

Other titles in this series:
**The Romans • The Saxons and Vikings
The Tudors • The Victorians**

Conceived and produced for Hodder Wayland by

Nutshell
MEDIA

Intergen House, 65–67 Western Road, Hove BN3 2JQ, UK
www.nutshellmedialtd.co.uk

© Copyright 2003 Nutshell Media

Editor: Polly Goodman
Designer: Simon Borrough
All reconstructions set up and photographed by: Martyn F. Chillmaid

First published in Great Britain in 2003 by Hodder Wayland,
an imprint of Hodder Children's Books.

This paperback edition published in 2005

Reprinted in 2007 by Wayland, an imprint of Hachette Children's Books.

British Library Cataloguing in Publication Data
Gogerly, Liz
The home front. – (Reconstructed)
1. World War, 1939–1945 – Social aspects – Great Britain – Pictorial works – Juvenile literature
2. Great Britain – Social conditions – 20th century – Pictorial works – Juvenile literature
I. Title
941'.08'0222

ISBN-13: 978 0 7502 4769 6

Printed and bound in China.

Hachette Children's Books
338 Euston Road, London NW1 3BH

Cover photographs: main photo: troops on the move; from top to bottom: an air-raid warden warns a
boy about an unexploded bomb; a family working on their allotment; inside a brick air-raid shelter;
ration books, clothing coupons, an identity card and other things to take on a shopping trip; evacuees at
a railway station.

Title page: A typical wartime kitchen.

Contents

Preparing for War

Spare wheel

Hard hat

Soft roof

Four-wheel-drive jeep

Throughout the Second World War, the streets were filled with troops on the move.

On 1 September 1939, Germany invaded Poland. Two days later Britain's Prime Minister, Neville Chamberlain, announced on the radio that Britain was at war with Germany. To many people, the news was no surprise. In 1938, Germany's leader, Adolf Hitler, had ordered the invasion of Austria and Czechoslovakia. He was hungry for more land and power in Europe. Britain and France had promised to help Poland if Hitler invaded. Once German planes began bombing Poland, Britain was forced to act. It was the start of the Second World War.

The First World War had been fought mainly on the ground. This time Britain had to prepare for a different kind of war – from the air. The German air force was likely to bomb British cities and strike at civilians.

Filter

Plastic window

Instructions

A girl practises putting on her gas mask. Fortunately, Hitler never dropped poisonous gas on Britain.

By early 1939, air-raid precautions had started. Thousands of leaflets were distributed, advising people how to make air-raid shelters in their homes. By September, 2 million steel shelters had been built, and black-out restrictions were also in place.

In 1938, 38 million gas masks had been issued to British civilians in case Hitler dropped bombs with poisonous gas on Britain. There were different kinds of masks for babies, children and adults. There were even masks for animals! Many people disliked having to carry their gas masks with them. Children had to take their masks to school, and some cinemas and theatres refused entrance to people who had forgotten their gas masks. In the first few weeks of war, schools, factories and other public places had gas-mask drills, so people would know what to do if there was a gas attack.

Many children hated putting the masks on. They felt tight and made it difficult to breathe. The smell of rubber and disinfectant made some people feel sick. Children found ways of having fun with their masks though – if they breathed out quickly they made rude noises!

Evacuation

Evacuees say their goodbyes before boarding a train at the station.

Gas mask box

Suitcases

Identity label

Luggage trolley

Guard

The British government was afraid that Germany would bomb London, Glasgow and other industrial cities, so it began organizing a mass evacuation of city-dwellers, called Operation Pied Piper. The aim was to protect the lives of mothers and children, and workers such as civil servants. Evacuees were to stay in the homes of ordinary people in safe areas of the countryside known as 'reception areas'. Each household that could provide a home for an evacuee was called a billet. On 1 September 1939, a few days before war was declared, Operation Pied Piper began.

About 1.5 million children between the ages of 5 and 14, and mothers of children under 5, travelled to their nearest railway station in Britain's major cities. Each child had to take a certain amount of clothes, a gas mask, and an identity label showing their name and address. The evacuees were packed on to specially organized trains and taken to reception areas. There they were appointed a suitable home.

Operation Pied Piper was hard for both the evacuees and host families who took them in. There were many stories of frightened young children, away from their families for the first time, who were placed in unfriendly homes. It wasn't easy for the host families either. Some were appalled when evacuees arrived from the city slums, hungry and dirty, with only one set of clothes.

By January 1940, when no German bombs had fallen on Britain, people began questioning the need for so many rules and regulations. Despite government warnings, over half of the evacuees had returned to their homes in the cities. But the threat of air raids had not gone away, so the government distributed leaflets and posters, urging people to remember safety and the war effort.

These government posters explain the importance of (from the left) evacuating to the countryside, carrying gas masks, and walking rather than using public transport.

Rationing

As soon as Britain joined the war, the Germans began attacking ships in the North Atlantic Ocean. These ships brought vital supplies of meat, fruit, vegetables and cereals to Britain from the USA, Canada and other countries. To make sure there would be enough food to go around, on 8 January 1940 the government introduced rationing of essential foods.

A typical grocer's shop during the war. Some of the food brands are still available today.

Food unavailable due to rationing

Air raid first-aid shelf

Goods weighed on scales

Fox's Glacier Mints

Bird's custard

Marmite stock cubes

4oz (113g) butter

2oz (56.5g) tea

4oz (113g) bacon

1 egg

1oz (28g) cheese

8oz (226g) sugar

Ration book

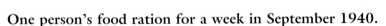

One person's food ration for a week in September 1940.

Each person was issued with a ration book containing coupons for their weekly allowance of certain foods. At first, only butter, sugar, bacon and ham were rationed. In March 1940, meat went on ration and in July, tea, margarine and cooking fats were also restricted. In the summer of 1940, German submarines sank more ships carrying food, and staple foods such as bread and fruit became in short supply, too.

Fortunately, in the spring of 1941, new foods started to appear on the shop shelves. Goods such as powdered eggs, soya flour, tinned, skimmed milk, and tinned meat called Spam were starting to arrive from the USA. Later, dehydrated meat was also imported, which was deboned and dried. The British housewife had to use her imagination if she was to turn these unusual foods into tasty meals for her family!

The ration of groceries for one person for a week would hardly make a decent breakfast for a hungry adult today. But rationing made sure that Britons didn't starve during the war. Not all foods were rationed. Bread was never rationed and the government decided against rationing sauces, and sweet and savoury spreads – the food was boring enough!

Wartime Wardrobe

In 1942, the government introduced clothes rationing to free up Britain's factories for making goods for the war. Clothes rationing meant that people had yet another ration book to take shopping. The Clothing Book contained 66 coupons that had to last each person 15 months. In that time, the coupons allowed a person to buy one complete outfit, including underwear and nightwear. A brand new coat might take 14 to 16 coupons, so the coupons had to be used wisely.

After clothes rationing was introduced, people had to make their clothes last longer. Government posters urged them to 'Make do and Mend', which meant repairing old clothes rather than throwing them away.

Faced with a shortage of clothes, people found interesting ways of making new outfits. Curtains were turned into children's clothes, and old blankets were sewn up to make new overcoats.

A girl passes a ladies' clothes shop, closed due to bomb damage.

Utility dress

Boarded-up window

Price list in coupons

10

There were even stories of brides getting married in dresses made from parachute silk. Stockings were almost impossible to find. As an alternative, many women covered their legs with gravy browning, and then got a friend to draw a line down the back of their legs with a black pen (for the seam). Make-up was also restricted, so soot from the chimney was used as eye-shadow, and red liquorice or beetroot juice could pass as lipstick.

The war affected the design of clothes as well as their production. Utility clothes were made from a limited range of material and designed to use less material. They were often plain and drab. Utility men's trousers were not allowed turn-ups and women's skirts were cut shorter, with fewer pleats and a regulated number of pockets and buttons. Hats were not rationed, so many women tried to make the best of themselves by wearing glamorous hats with feathers and ribbons.

On shopping trips, people had to remember to take their ration books, coupons and identity cards, as well as their money.

Identity card

Child's ration book

Postage stamp

Clothing ration book and coupons

Money and bus tickets

Food ration book

Dig for Victory!

Before the war, Britain imported nearly 80 per cent of its fruit and many of its vegetables. When the war began, Britain suddenly had to provide for itself. In the summer of 1939, government posters and leaflets encouraged people to 'grow their own'. Lawns and flower beds were turned into vegetable patches, and disused land became allotments. In their gardens, people began to grow potatoes, carrots, onions, and other vegetables that grew quickly and easily.

A father and his children work on their allotment. The government urged people to get their vitamins from home-grown vegetables instead of fruit.

| Hoe | Onions | Potatoes | Cabbages | Bucket |

In 1940, the government launched the 'Dig for Victory' campaign, and gave awards to people if they grew vegetables all year round. Everybody got behind the campaign. Children trooped down to the allotments after school. With many men away fighting, women also got to work with their spades. All kinds of vegetables were grown, including parsnips, peppers, marrows and peas.

People found new and unusual places to grow their food. Soil was poured over air-raid shelters and vegetable seeds were sown on the roofs. Runner beans and beetroot were grown on football pitches, tennis courts and railway sidings. People grew tomatoes and herbs on their window-sills, and mushrooms inside their dark, damp air-raid shelters. The gardens at Windsor Castle and Buckingham Palace, and even the moat at the Tower of London, were all turned into vegetable patches.

Keeping people well-nourished was another way of helping Britain to win the war. In advertising campaigns, the government told people to eat their vegetables so they would get all the vitamins they needed. In leaflets, cartoon characters such as 'Potato Pete' and 'Doctor Carrot' explained the nutritional value of vegetables.

The government issued colourful posters to remind people on the home front of the ways in which they could help. 'Dig for Victory' is one of the most memorable slogans from the war.

The Kitchen Front

Rationing meant that housewives had to be inventive with the ingredients they were allowed to buy. Help was at hand though, and every morning a radio programme called *The Kitchen Front* offered recipes and advice about food. Instead of sugar, cooks used beetroot, carrots and parsnips to make puddings or jam. To save butter, pastry was made from potatoes, and dripping was smeared on bread.

Wasting food was frowned upon during the war, and leaflets and posters proclaimed: 'Food is a munition of war, DON'T WASTE IT.' People caught throwing out stale bread or the edible parts of vegetables were told off by the council.

Vegetable peelings and other food scraps would be fed to pigs or rabbits.

Rabbit and onions

Cabbage

Toaster

Gas oven

Gas fridge

A selection of foods eaten during the war years.

A popular saying was that the only part of a pig that couldn't be eaten was its squeal. Meat was an important source of protein, so the whole of the pig, including its trotters and tail was eaten. Other cheap cuts of meat such as tripe, mutton and kidneys were flavoured with herbs to make them more tasty.

To supplement their diets, some people reared chickens, rabbits or pigs in their gardens. Others banded together to form a 'pig club'. They would give all their food scraps and leftovers to a farmer to feed a pig. Later, when the pig was killed, the club members were given some of its meat.

Many people complained about the food during the war, but most people had actually never eaten so well. Nowadays we recognize that a diet rich in fruit and vegetables, and low in sugar, fat and animal products is better for our health. Some nutritionists even suggest that the home front diet was healthier and more nutritious than the food we eat today.

Cabbage

Dripping

Liver and kidney

Tripe and onions

Recipe for dried eggs

Pig's trotter and tail, lard and caul

15

Everyday Living

Life on the home front was very busy. There were vegetable allotments to tend during the day and clothes to make and mend. Every night, each household had to go through the lengthy process of checking that their black-out curtains were drawn properly. One small chink of light showing at any window was enough to attract a loud rap on the door from an angry air-raid warden.

During the war most people went to bed early, but not before listening to the BBC nine o'clock news on the radio. After France surrendered to Germany, between half and two-thirds of the British population regularly tuned in to this news update. Other popular radio broadcasts were the speeches of the Prime Minister, Winston Churchill, who came to power in 1940. In his deep, gruff voice he delivered words of encouragement to Britons everywhere.

Another quiet night at home during the black-out.

Wireless set   Hand sewing machine

Jigsaw puzzle   Coal fire

Knitting   Newspaper

Stylus

Radio tuning knobs

Record

A father puts a record on the radiogram, a combined radio and record player.

Apart from the news, the radio broadcast lots of programmes to cheer people up. There was *Children's Hour*, when children could enjoy the company of characters such as 'Larry the Lamb' and 'Dennis the Dachshund'. There were comedy shows, dance music, and songs by Vera Lynn, Gracie Fields and George Formby. Songs like 'We'll Meet Again' and 'The White Cliffs of Dover' by Vera Lynn became popular, but cheekier songs like 'Yes, We Have No Bananas' and 'Roll Out the Barrel' were favourites too – especially in sing-alongs in the air-raid shelters. Going to the cinema was another way in which people could escape their homes. Hollywood films like *Gone with the Wind* helped people to forget about the war.

Women's Work

Life in the women's services promised freedom and adventure, and in the first months of the war, 43,000 women volunteered to join up. They could choose between the women's branch of the army, called the Auxiliary Territorial Service (ATS), the Women's Auxiliary Air Force (WAAF) or the Women's Royal Navy (WRN, or Wrens).

At first, many women didn't get the adventure they craved because their jobs were in administration or in the kitchens. Later in the war their roles became more varied. Members of the WAAF were radio-operators, photographers, mechanics and ferry pilots. Women in the army operated anti-aircraft batteries, although they were only supposed to aim the guns at the enemy and were not allowed to shoot. When Princess Elizabeth (now Queen Elizabeth II) joined the ATS she became a driver and learned about mechanics.

A member of the Women's Royal Army Corps (WRAC).

A housewife puts some wet washing through a mangle to squeeze out the water.

Mangle

Wash boiler

Electric iron

Pegs

Housewives had an important part to play in the war, too. Posters and radio broadcasts urged them to 'keep the home fires burning'. Many daily chores were more difficult because people were told to be less wasteful. On wash day, women had to use less coal and electricity, and soap was rationed. Women also had to look after evacuees, or mind the children of women who were working in the factories.

Women who still wanted to do more for the war effort joined a voluntary group. The Women's Voluntary Service (WVS) ran canteens and mobile kitchens, which fed rescue workers and victims in bombed areas. In the countryside, the Women's Institute (WI) produced tonnes of canned fruit and jam, and the Women's Land Army (WLA) helped on the farms.

Children's War

Everyone wanted to do their bit for the war, and children were no exception. They became collectors of household salvage. During the war, the government ran hundreds of appeals to collect metal, glass, clothes and paper for recycling. In 1940, the government appealed for more aluminium: 'We will turn your pots and pans into Spitfires and Hurricanes,' they said, and everybody was inspired. Children sacrificed their old metal toys or bikes for this latest appeal.

Jam jars

Wheelbarrow

Clothes

Saucepan

To encourage children to collect more salvage, the government formed a club called Cogs. Children who did well were awarded badges. Most items were recycled, but unfortunately great piles of scrap metal were left to rust because there was enough scrap metal to build aircraft already.

Children pushed wheelbarrows from door to door, collecting anything that could be recycled.

In wartime Britain it was dangerous for children to play out in the street. Bombs had left partially destroyed houses that could suddenly collapse without warning. The black-out restrictions meant that there were no fairground attractions and Guy Fawkes' Night was banned for the whole of the war. When children did go out they were told to stay close to home and out of harm's way. This meant entertaining themselves with anything they could find. If they were lucky, they might come across one of the most prized souvenirs of the war – bits of metal from shot-down German planes.

At home, children had new games and comics to keep them entertained. Comics like *The Beano* and *The Dandy* featured German cartoon characters called 'Nasty Nazis', and a hero called Desperate Dan. Games such as Bomber Command, Air Sea Rescue, ARP and River Plate meant children got a taste of the war in their own front room. One of the most popular games was darts, with Adolf Hitler as the bulls-eye.

Children made up games using things they found on the streets.

Air Raid!

The first German air raid took place in London on the evening of 7 September 1940. Within months, Liverpool, Birmingham, Coventry and other cities were hit, too. At the beginning of the war, the government had built brick shelters and distributed Anderson shelters to protect people during air raids. In London, people also sheltered in the London Underground.

(Right) Another long night in a brick air-raid shelter.

(Below) A boy falls asleep under a Morrison shelter.

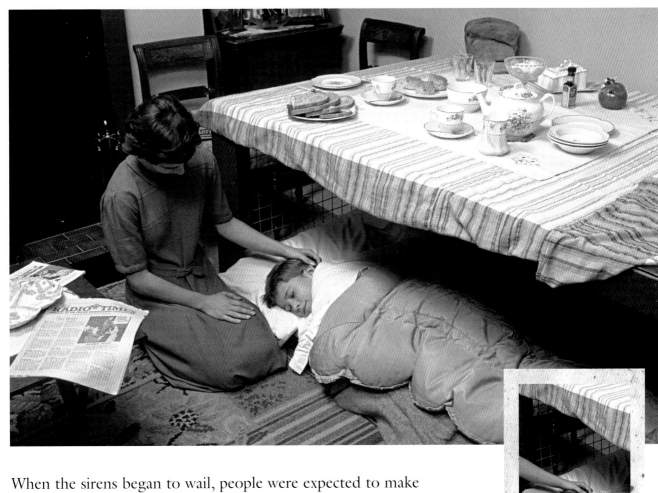

When the sirens began to wail, people were expected to make their way to their nearest air-raid shelter, but many stayed at home. The Anderson shelters were dark and damp, and the brick shelters were not very safe. Despite air-raid precautions, 60 per cent of the British population decided to stay at home during bomb attacks. In 1941, the government introduced Morrison shelters. These large, steel tables were usually put in people's living rooms and provided protection for two adults and two children. They meant that people could stay safely at home during an attack.

Wire mesh

Steel top used as a table

The Blitz

An air-raid warden searches for survivors in a bombed-out house.

Night after night, from September 1940 until May 1941, German bombers attacked British cities, ports and industrial areas. In London, the Blitz went on for 57 nights in a row. Thousands of people were killed, and homes, offices, shops and factories were reduced to rubble. In November 1940, the town of Coventry and its cathedral were destroyed. Hitler hoped that he could bring the British public's spirits so low that Britain would surrender, but he under-estimated Britain's defiance.

Despite the air raids, the British attitude was 'business as usual'. Many people walked to work through rubble-filled streets, and businesses kept going even if their offices had been hit. But it was the work of the rescue services that kept the situation under control. Air-raid wardens, the fire service, the police, medical staff and ambulance workers worked in terrible conditions, risking their own lives to save the lives of others.

Air-raid warden

Torch

Bomb

One in every ten bombs that fell was a 'dud', which meant that it did not explode on impact. But some bombs had a delayed action fuse, which meant they could go off at any time. These bombs were called UXBs (unexploded bombs). People living within 500 metres of a UXB had to be evacuated until the bomb had been safely defused.

UXBs caused great upheaval, but the most frightening bombs to hit Britain were the V1 and V2 missiles, which Hitler used from June to September 1944. In London alone, 6,000 people were killed and 24,000 injured during this period. People flocked back to the air-raid shelters to avoid these deadly bombs, which were so quiet that people didn't hear them until they exploded. But Hitler's desperate last attempt to break the British spirit had come too late – the Allies were winning the war.

An air-raid warden warns a boy about an unexploded bomb.

Sandbags

Danger sign and barrier

Air-raid warden

A New Britain

On 8 May 1945, Britain celebrated Victory in Europe (VE) Day and people partied all day and all night. That evening the street-lights were switched on again for the first time since the war had begun. When the celebrations were over, people started looking forward to a new Britain.

One of the first problems for the government was housing. During the war, nearly 500,000 houses had been destroyed. New homes were also needed for the 2 million people who had got married during the war. Prefabricated houses were the answer. These simple homes were made from recycled metal from wartime salvage. By January 1948, almost 160,000 'prefabs' had been built. The life of each house was supposed to be just 10 years, but at only £1,300 to build, they were a cheap and easy solution to the housing problem.

Prefab houses were delivered from the factory in sections and could be erected in about four hours.

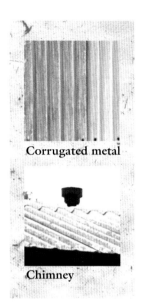

Corrugated metal

Chimney

To many families, prefabs were a 'step up'. Before the war, many people lived in homes with no bathroom or inside toilet, no central heating, and a backyard rather than a garden. The simple prefab had all the mod cons. The bathroom had hot running water. The modern fitted kitchen had a sink and a larder. It also came with a gas fridge and an electric stove. A solid fuel fire in the living room provided enough heat to be piped through to the two bedrooms and heat water in the bathroom.

All prefabs had a garden and were usually in estates, so there was a great sense of community. Most families were delighted with their new homes, and the humble little prefab became so popular that many were still in use 40 years after they were first built.

Prefab bathrooms had the luxury of an inside toilet and hot running water.

Hot running water

Rationed shaving soap

Timeline

1938 The British government begins
issuing gas masks.

1939

July All British men aged 20 are called
up to join the armed forces.

1 Sept Germany invades Poland.

Black-out restrictions are started
in Britain.

Operation Pied Piper, the mass
evacuation programme, begins.

3 Sept Britain, France, Australia and New
Zealand declare war on Germany.

Petrol is rationed.

1940

8 Jan Bacon, ham, sugar and butter
are rationed.

March Meat is rationed.

9 Apr Germany invades Norway and
Denmark.

10 May Germany invades the Netherlands,
Luxembourg, Belgium and France.

Winston Churchill replaces Neville
Chamberlain as Prime Minister
of Britain.

22 May The Emergency Powers Law is
passed, which puts all British citizens
at the disposal of the British
government.

26 May British and French servicemen are
–3 June evacuated from Dunkirk, in France.

27 May All British men aged over 26 are
called up to join the armed forces.

10 July The Battle of Britain begins.

Sept The Battle of Britain ends and
Germany begins to attack British
cities.

7 Sept The London Blitz begins.

14 Nov Coventry is devastated during a
German air raid.

1941

6 Apr Germany invades Yugoslavia and
Greece.

May Cheese and jam are rationed.
The Blitz ends.

2 June Clothes rationing is introduced.

22 June Germany invades Russia.

1 July Coal restrictions are introduced.

11 Dec Germany and Italy declare war on
the USA.

1942

26 Jan The first American GIs arrive in
Britain.

Feb Soap is rationed.

Apr The Germans start bombing the
historic towns of Exeter, Norwich,
York, Canterbury and Bath.

1943

31 Jan The Germans surrender at
Stalingrad, USSR.

3 May All British women aged between
18 and 45 have to sign up for
part-time war work.

10 July British, US and Canadian troops
launch the Allied invasion of Sicily.

1944

6 June D-Day landings in France.

13 June The first V1 missile hits Britain.

8 Sept The first V2 missile hits Britain.

17 Sept The 'dim-out' replaces the black-out
in Britain.

1945

8 May The Allies capture Berlin and declare
Victory in Europe.

Glossary

Allies Countries that have made an agreement to work together towards a common goal. During the Second World War, Britain, the USA, the USSR and France were allies.

allotment A piece of land for growing vegetables.

allowance A fixed amount of something that is given for a purpose.

Anderson shelter An air-raid shelter made from corrugated iron, which was buried in people's gardens.

black-out The period between the hours of darkness, when lights had to be put out or covered.

The Blitz The German air raids against Britain from 1940–41.

brands Names of foods given to them by the company that makes them.

civilians Ordinary citizens who are not members of the armed forces.

civil servants People who work for the government.

drill A method of remembering something by practising it many times, for example, practising how to react during an emergency.

dripping Fat collected from boiled or roasted beef.

evacuation The movement of people to an area of safety.

evacuees People who have been evacuated.

ferry pilots Pilots who take planes from the factory to the airfield but are not involved in military combat.

gas mask A mask that covers the eyes, nose and mouth, and filters out poisonous gas.

host families Ordinary people living in the countryside who provided homes for evacuees.

London Underground The network of underground trains in London, otherwise known as 'the Tube'.

Morrison shelter A steel structure that looked like a table and was designed to protect people during an air raid.

munition Military equipment, including ammunition.

nutrional value The amount of nourishment in food.

rationing The restriction of goods such as food, clothing and fuel, so that they can be shared out equally.

regulated Controlled or restricted.

salvage Old or unwanted objects that can be recycled.

slogan A short, catchy phrase used in advertising.

Spam The brand name of a tinned meat product made mainly from ham.

staple foods The main foods that make up a diet.

tripe The stomach-lining of an ox.

trotters Animal feet when they are used as food.

utility clothes Clothes designed for their usefulness rather than their appearance.

Activities

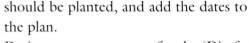

pp4–5 Preparing for War

- Visit your local library and look at local newspapers printed on 11 November, Remembrance Day, for the last few years. Look for stories about brave people who fought in the war.
- On your next visit to a local or national museum, look out for old gas masks. Write a list of instructions explaining how to use one.

pp6–7 Evacuation

- Find and read the book *Carrie's War* by Nina Bawden in your local library. Write a play about evacuation with other members of your class.
- Imagine that you are an evacuee. Write a diary over a week.

pp8–9 Rationing

- Visit your local library and look at local newspapers from 1939–42. Look for articles about the introduction of rationing, or recipes and advice about food.
- Plan a weekly menu for a family of four using rationed food and other kinds of food that were available during the war.

pp10–11 Wartime Wardrobe

- Visit second-hand bookshops or car boot sales and look for magazines, books or sewing patterns from the Second World War. Compare the home front fashions with those today.
- Design a ration book that contains clothing coupons.

pp12–13 Dig for Victory!

- Draw a plan of a vegetable patch, marking the position of the different vegetables. Find out when the seeds for each vegetable should be planted, and add the dates to the plan.
- Design your own poster for the 'Dig for Victory' campaign.

pp14–15 The Kitchen Front

- Interview as many people as you can who lived during the war. Find out the most unusual food that they ate. Make a chart listing the unusual foods, from the most disgusting at the top to the tastiest at the bottom.
- Using the food described on page 15, write a menu for a dinner party during the Second World War.

pp16–17 Everyday Living

- Watch some old films made during the Second World War. Hunt for films like *Mrs Miniver* and *Casablanca*. Look at the clothes in the films and compare them with the clothes on page 10.
- Imagine you have travelled back in time to a home during the Second World War. Write a letter to a friend describing a typical evening.

pp18–19 Women's Work

- Imagine you have just joined the Women's Royal Navy. Write a diary describing your first day.
- Make a chart listing the kitchen appliances you can see in the photograph on page 19. Describe how each appliance has changed since the 1940s.

pp20–21 Children's War

- In a role play with members of your class, collect salvage from your neighbours. Assign roles of pushing the wheelbarrow, knocking on doors and sorting the salvage.

- In second-hand bookshops and car boot fairs, hunt for old children's comics, annuals and books from the war. Compare the style of writing and pictures to today's comics.

pp22–23 Air Raid!
- Write a set of instructions for what to do in an air raid, a little like what to do in the event of a fire.
- Find out if there are any old air-raid shelters still surviving in your local area. Some people still have an old Anderson shelter in their garden – see if you can find one near you.

pp24–25 The Blitz
- Write a short play about a family who leave London for the weekend only to return to find their house flattened by a bomb.

Make up dialogue for each of the characters, then act out the play.
- Visit your local library and look at local newspapers from 1940–41, and 1944–45. Find out if bombs were dropped in your local area. If so, visit the places that were bombed and look at the buildings there now. Which buildings do you think survived the war and which were built after the war?

pp26–27 A New Britain
- Visit your local Record Office and ask to look at maps of your area from 1945–50. Look at where new houses were built and find out if any of these were prefabricated houses. Find out if there are any prefab houses still existing in your area.

Finding Out More

Books to Read
At Home in World War Two: The Blitz; Evacuation; Rationing; Women's War; At Work; Propaganda by Stewart Ross (Evans, 2001 and 2004)

Britain at War: Air Raids; Evacuation; Rationing; Women's War by Martin Parsons (Hodder Wayland, 2000)

Carrie's War by Nina Bawden (Puffin, 1993)

My War: Evacuee by Peter Hepplewhite (Hodder Wayland, 2005)

Goodnight Mr Tom by Michelle Magorian (Longman, 2000)

Horrible History: The Blitzed Brits by Terry Deary (Scholastic, 2004)

The Past in Pictures: The Home Front by Fiona Reynoldson (Hodder Wayland, 2002)

The World Wars: The Home Front in World Wars II by Pat Levy (Hodder Wayland, 2003)

Places to Visit
The Imperial War Museum, Lambeth Road, London SE1 6HZ
The original propaganda posters that appear in this book are held at this museum, which produces many educational packs on the home front in the Second World War.

Avoncroft Museum of Historic Buildings, Stoke Heath, Bromsgrove, Worcestershire B60 4JR
Many of the photographs that appear in this book, including the ration books and the prefab house, were taken at this fascinating museum.

Flambards Village Theme Park, Helston, Cornwall TR13 0QA
The photographs of the grocer's shop, Morrison shelter, and the air-raid warden and child were taken at this theme park.

Index